AF284548

Overcome your Fear of Contact

A Training Program:

In Seven Steps from Fear of Contact to a Social Butterfly

Anne Schlosser

Bibliografische Information der Deutschen Nationalbibliothek:

Die Deutsche Nationalbibliothek verzeichnet diese Publikation in der Deutschen Nationalbibliografie; detaillierte bibliografische Daten sind im Internet über http://dnb.dnb.de abrufbar.

© 2020, Anne Schlosser, 2nd Edition

Herstellung und Verlag: BoD – Books on Demand, Norderstedt

ISBN: 978-3-7519-8487-4

Introduction

By using this book, you accept this disclaimer in full.

No advice

The book contains information. The information is not advice and should not be treated as such.

No representations or warranties

To the maximum extent permitted by applicable law and subject to section below, we exclude all representations, warranties, undertakings and guarantees relating to the book.

Without prejudice to the generality of the foregoing paragraph, we do not represent, warrant, undertake or guarantee:

- that the information in the book is correct, accurate, complete or non-misleading.

- that the use of the guidance in the book will lead to any particular outcome or result.

Limitations and exclusions of liability

The limitations and exclusions of liability set out in this section and elsewhere in this disclaimer: are subject to section 6 below; and govern all liabilities arising under the disclaimer or in relation to the book, including liabilities arising in contract, in tort (including negligence) and for breach of statutory duty.

We will not be liable to you in respect of any losses arising out of any event or events beyond our reasonable control.

We will not be liable to you in respect of any business losses, including without limitation loss of or damage to profits, income, revenue, use, production, anticipated savings, business, contracts, commercial opportunities or goodwill.

We will not be liable to you in respect of any loss or corruption of any data, database or software.

We will not be liable to you in respect of any special, indirect or consequential loss or damage.

Exceptions

Nothing in this disclaimer shall: limit or exclude our liability for death or personal injury resulting from negligence; limit or exclude our liability for fraud or fraudulent misrepresentation; limit any of our liabilities in any way that is not permitted under applicable law; or exclude any of our liabilities that may not be excluded under applicable law.

Severability

If a section of this disclaimer is determined by any court or other competent authority to be unlawful and/or unenforceable, the other sections of this disclaimer continue in effect.

If any unlawful and/or unenforceable section would be lawful or enforceable if part of it were deleted, that part will be deemed to be deleted, and the rest of the section will continue in effect.

Law and jurisdiction

This disclaimer will be governed by and construed in accordance with Swiss law, and any disputes relating to this disclaimer will be subject to the exclusive jurisdiction of the courts of Switzerland.

Inhaltsverzeichnis

Inhaltsverzeichnis **9**

Foreword **11**

The Program **13**

Step 1: "Please smile." **14**

Step 2: "Say it out loud: Hallo". **17**

Step 3: "How do I get to ...?" **20**

Step 4: "What time is it now?" **22**

Step 5: "Can you please switch"? **24**

Step 6: Make compliments **27**

Step 7: The recommendation Question **30**

The Easy Version **32**

End of training? **34**

Foreword

Most people limit themselves with negative self-beliefs. For most of our lives we can talk, but the idea of approaching a stranger makes us afraid. The ability to speak in front of several people causes panic. I myself was quite similar. When I was to speak for the first time to a couple of strangers, I spent three sleepless nights, suffered during the lecture while sweating and almost peed in my pants. But I survived it. Now, I speak regularly before several hundred people and have fun doing it.

I have developed the seven steps outlined here based on my own developments and my experiences. The program allows you to perform it without the assistance of a trainer. It is only important that you are honest with yourself. Only go to the next step, when you really "feel good" with the previous words.

I wish you lots of fun on your personal way to more interesting contacts, zest for life and professional success.

Yours Anne Schlosser

The Program

The following program is designed so that you can work through it unaided. With each step you achieve, record the best results and your experiences in the form of a small success diary. Every night, make yourself write to keep account: What have you done in order to reach the next step? What successes you have achieved and what are your findings from this? Also keep in account where you see chances to improve yourself in. You should also allow yourself to experiment, to achieve better results.

If you notice that in the course of your training that your results deteriorate, refer to your success diary that reports on past days, when you were particularly successful, and check what you have changed since then. This way, you have the best chance of finding further success.

Step 1: "Please smile."

Let us simply begin with the training: Smile at people. I'm not talking about a smile so forced that it can hold the person you are communicating with in doubt of an expression of a toothache. I speak of a warm smile that the other can actually believe in.

How are the reactions? I would love to tell you that people smile back. The reality is very different. In my experience, about only 10 percent of the people who you smile at, will smile back. Others will look the other way or make gestures that look like they are questioning your mental competence. No Matter. Smile at people.

You can prepare for it by practicing at home in front of the bathroom mirror (or the make-up mirror). Smile at the people you meet the same way as you did smiling at the mirror. If your reflection does not return recognizable smiles, you should change something about your smile.

Without wishing to sound esoteric: You can experiment with your smile. If you smile at a person as described, concentrate on something you might like about this person. Although you do not know these people, you may quietly speculate. Next, try to present this sympathy in the smile. You will find that in many cases the reactions are different.

In step 1, you will learn the following things:

- Reach out with an open smile at people, as it will help you in communication. It breaks down boundaries and signals your counterpart sympathy and openness.

- You will experience a huge influence on what you think about the person you are speaking to, and a type of communication you can have, even if you do not express it verbally.

- You will gain more self-confidence, already trying where ever possible to speak with a stranger or you can learn to handle rejection and realize that it is not so bad.

The Goal:

You have successfully mastered the first step, when more than seven unknown people smile back at you in one day. It is ideal that during this first step (or one of the following) you get into a positive conversation with people.

Step 2: "Say it out loud: Hallo".

Now let us increase the difficulty a little. - Or is it perhaps not difficult? In step 2, you have to greet strangers. Whether you say "Hello," "Hey", "Howdy" or "Hi,": It is not about the language, but only the fact that you greeted a total stranger. Depending on where you live, the reaction may be different. In the countryside your greeting will tend to be more replied than in the city.

When I did this exercise for the first time, I experienced people who greeted me back, those who shook their heads, and one or the other, who asked if we knew each other. I came in contact with a few people and two of them became business partners in my downline later.

Again, I recommend that you use the extra exercise with positive thoughts from step 1. You will see the results are thus significantly better. People feel, whether we are dealing with them "with good meaning", and react accordingly.

Of course there were also the negative reactions again. This is normal and part of the training. You should learn that negative reactions are "no doomsday" and have nothing to do with you. Be thankful to these people because you learn through their refusal not to take such reactions personally.

In Step 2, you will learn the following things:

- Simple contact changing with unknown people

You gain experience with positive and negative reactions and learn to deal with negative reactions.

The Goal:

You have reached your goal, when in one day seven (or more) people greet you back in a friendly manner. Once you've done that, you can go to step. 3

Step 3: "How do I get to ...?"

While our steps of making contact with others were relatively non-binding, we now take a step, where you significantly bring further your goal to start a conversation with people. Now it comes to interacting with an unfamiliar person.

Your task is simple: Go to people and ask them for directions. If you live in a small town, it would make more sense if you go to the nearest large town, so that the people will not feel fooled.

In step 3, you will learn the following things:

- To talk to a person and ask them for something

- Successfully carry out a first brief interaction with a stranger person

You gain self-confidence to response to strangers and gain experience on how you act.

The Goal:

You have successfully done this step if you have had a consultation five times in one day. "Do not know", "I'm not from around here" and similar responses are of course not counted as information.

Step 4: "What time is it now?"

Meanwhile, you were able to record some successes. Now we go a step further and try to specially create a conversation. We do this with the question of time.

Ask strangers for the time. Some people will be happy to tell it to you, others will not respond and leave you standing. Still, others will tell you that they have no watch. Exactly these are important for our exercise. Ask back if these people may have a mobile phone that tells the time. If yes, ask the stranger to briefly look it up for you.

In this task, you should wear neither a watch nor have a cell phone with you.

In step 4, you will learn the following things:

- You begin to systematically lead the conversation and ask the person about concrete things. Also keep them on a hook, instead of being satisfied with the first answer.

- Your self-confidence in the interaction with strangers grow.

The Goal:

You have successfully passed this step if you managed to ask at least seven people in one day for the time. Ideally, as many of them who specially brought out their cell phones just to tell you the time.

Step 5:
"Can you please switch"?

You now have first-hand experience in interacting with strangers. Now it comes to the next challenge: "Can you give me X change, please?" is the next step. Ask on the streets if anyone could change for you 5 euros or Swiss francs to smaller pocket change. Then you have to ask the next person if they can change your many coins for a 5 euro note or a 5-franc piece.

Most people go for it relatively easy when you are willing to trade notes instead of coins. It corresponds to what you know from their lives. People will change large notes for coins to buy beverages or purchase tickets at the parking ticket machines. However, if you ask for the reverse, as in to get out of small change a larger unit, it will leave many people puzzled.

When I do this exercise with new members of a team, it always comes to the same question: "What can I say, and why do I need to change my coins to bills?"

A new partner even recently expressed suspicion: "They will think that I want to give him fake money." My question is, from where she came to this thought and whether she has had experience in this type of situation that made her say no. The opinion simply sprang from their belief.

My experience in this exercise is that most people do not ask. If they do, then you can give any explanation such as that of the machine you wish to use just accepts only the relevant banknotes or coins. The type of feedback in this step also depends on how convincing you are. If you ask nicely and with a smile expressed, and your appurtenance already has deep conviction that you need the changed money, then you will be successful in the majority of cases.

In Step 5, you will learn the following things:

- how kindly you ask for a favour
- how to bring your appreance to be convincing and to fit what you say, how you can get people to fulfill your request happily.

The Goal:

You have reached the goal of this step if you have, in a day, changed your coins into a larger unit at least five times (f.ex. 1 $ to coins or back).

Step 6: Make compliments

In step 6, we are working on another competency, which will help us in communicating with others. People can defend themselves against almost anything, but hardly against an honest-meant compliment. Those that make such compliments at us, are to us sympathetic. We see them with a positive vibration. The condition is that the speaker must be taken seriously. Most people have a very fine sensorium, which shows us, if anyone thinks a compliment is true or if it is only expressed in order to achieve something. Be the person you are speaking to and express sincere compliments only.

When we look at a person with sympathy, we can always find something positive in them. Examples of compliments can be:

- Your hairstyle fits great to your type. Could you recommend your hairdresser to me?

- I just saw your beautiful brooch. Is this an opal in the middle?

I must absolutely congratulate you on your clothes. The sitting is so great. Is it custom-made?

Avoid platitudes and pick-up lines. If you are a man and you say to a young woman "Your eyes shine like stars', then that is not necessarily taken as positive. In the examples I have provided, the compliment adds directly to a question. Firstly, the whole works as a natural complement and the question is added to help in a further discussion.

In step 6, you will learn the following things:

- to focus on positive aspects and attributes of people

- To address people on positive attributes and make compliments

Specifically to get into a conversation with people

The Goal:

The objective of this training step is achieved when you have succeeded in getting into a conversation in three different situations in a day with three different, unfamiliar people, after you have addressed them with a compliment.

Step 7:
The recommendation Question

The final step of your training is about asking an unknown person for a recommendation. Talk to a stranger and ask them, for example, for a restaurant where you can have lunch well, or for a nice place to walk. I liked to do this exercise while traveling to learn about more beautiful places that are not in the guide books. You can also ask for a hairdresser etc.

Here you will hopefully see how interesting talking can be, if you go with an interest in other people. Not because you want to offer them something or to convince them of your "wisdom", but because it is simply thrilling to listen to someone and to focus on what the person has to say.

Even if many professional sellers do not want to admit it: In business, it is not a matter of talking people over until they sign a contract as in an act of convincing, but rather to listen to people with an interest and, where possible, solve problems.

In step 7, you will learn the following things:

- reach out to other people with interest

- a willingness to listen to other people

- appreciation of the statements of others

- to start interesting discussions based on the statements of the person you are speaking with.

The Easy Version

It may be that a few of the seven steps make you feel fear. Or you feel uncomfortable in some way. This is quite normal. But to overcome this lump in your stomach is precisely the goal of this training. Only if you work very concretely by exceeding the limits of your comfort zone and to extend it, can you "grow", learn new things and finally get out of having fear of contact to enjoying contact with people.

If you still find one or the other training steps particularly difficult, I suggest that you practice it at a networking event. In almost every region there XING groups or networking organizations such as BNI (Business Network International), where people meet to network. Here you will receive less negative reactions and may try to get in contact with others. People come to these events to find business partners, and are generally happy if they do not have to make the first move.

This light-version can perhaps be essential in aiding you with one or the other steps in your development and give you courage for the next step. However, you should be aware that it is necessary to achieve these goals to achieve success in "the wild", that is, out on the streets and anywhere in everyday life. Only that will help you sustainably advance.

End of training?

You have now successfully completed the seven steps of your training to overcome the fear of contact. Congratulations! This will open many doors for you in your professional and private life.

For one of my partners, the door opening went so far that he is now engaged to a person who he had made a compliment on (step 6).

I really hope that the training also brings joy and many successful experiences for you. But do not forget: practice makes perfect. Even after you have gone through the training, it pays off to have days of repetitions and to pull off all of the steps consistently.

I would be delighted if you leave an online feed-back with your experiences and successes with the training.

Yours Anne Schlosser